NEIL ARMSTRONG

First Man on the Moon

Jane Bingham

FACT CAT

Get your paws on this fantastic new mega-series from Wayland!

Join our Fact Cat on a journey of fun learning about every subject under the sun!

Published in paperback in 2016 by Wayland
© Wayland 2016

Wayland
An imprint of
Hachette Children's Group
Part of Hodder & Stoughton
Carmelite House
50 Victoria Embankment
London EC4Y 0DZ

Produced for Wayland by
White-Thomson Publishing Ltd
www.wtpub.co.uk
+44 (0) 843 208 7460

Editor: Jane Bingham
Design: Rocket Design (East Anglia) Ltd
Fact Cat illustrations: Shutterstock/Julien Troneur
Other illustrations: Stefan Chabluk
Consultant: Kate Ruttle

A catalogue for this title is available from the British Library

ISBN: 978 0 7502 9042 5
eBook ISBN: 978 0 7502 9041 8

Dewey Number: 629.4'5'0092-dc23
10 9 8 7 6 5 4 3 2

Wayland is a division of Hachette Children's Books,
an Hachette UK company.
www.hachette.co.uk

Printed and bound in China

Picture and illustration credits:
Stefan Chabluk 12; Wikimedia 1, 4, 5, 6 (top), 8, 10, 11, 12, 13, 14, 15, 16, 17, 18, 19, 20, 21; pixelsnap/Shutterstock 6 (bottom); Kumina Studios/Shutterstock 7; mrHanson/Shutterstock 9.

Every effort has been made to clear copyright.
Should there be any inadvertent omission,
please apply to the publisher for rectification.

The author, Jane Bingham, is a writer and editor specialising in children's educational publishing.

The consultant, Kate Ruttle, is a literacy expert and SENCO, and teaches in Suffolk.

FACT CAT FACT

There is a question for you to answer on each spread in this book. You can check your answers on page 24.

CONTENTS

WHO WAS NEIL ARMSTRONG?

Neil Armstrong was an American **astronaut**. He was the first person to walk on the Moon.

Armstrong wore a special spacesuit for his Moon walk. It allowed him to breathe and walk around. How long did his Moon walk last?

When Armstrong stepped onto the Moon, he said "That's one small step for a man, one giant leap for **mankind**."

The second man on the Moon was Buzz Aldrin. Armstrong took this photo of him.

FACT CAT FACT

There is no **oxygen** on the Moon. This means no animals or plants can live there.

YOUNG NEIL

Neil Armstrong was born in 1930 in the state of Ohio, USA. He was the oldest of three children. His family moved home many times while he was growing up.

Neil with his sister June

Young Neil was a keen Boy Scout. He passed many tests and became an Eagle Scout. The Eagle Scout badge is the highest **award** for American Scouts.

Neil started learning to fly when he was 15. The next year, he took his flying test. He gained his **pilot**'s **licence** before he passed his driving test!

When Neil was five years old he had a ride on a plane like this. At that time, planes had been flying for just over 30 years. Can you find out the date of the first plane flight?

FACT CAT **FACT**

Armstrong took his Scout badge on his flight to the Moon.

BECOMING AN ASTRONAUT

When Armstrong was 17, he went to **university**. He studied how planes fly. Then he joined the **navy** as a pilot. He served in the US Navy for four years.

After he left the navy, Armstrong became a test pilot. He tested out new planes to make sure they were safe.

In 1958, Armstrong joined the US **Space Program**. At that time, the USA and Russia were **competing** in the **Space Race**. Both countries wanted to send a man into space.

In 1961, a Russian astronaut became the first man to travel in space. He was called Yuri Gagarin. What was the name of his spacecraft?

FACT CAT FACT

The first woman went into space in 1963. She was a Russian astronaut called Valentina Tereshkova.

PROJECT GEMINI

By the 1960s, the Russians were winning the Space Race. This made the Americans very keen to get ahead. In 1962, they began work on Project Gemini. The aim of the project was to prepare for a Moon landing.

Neil Armstrong was one of the Gemini astronauts. Before he went into space, he was given many medical tests.

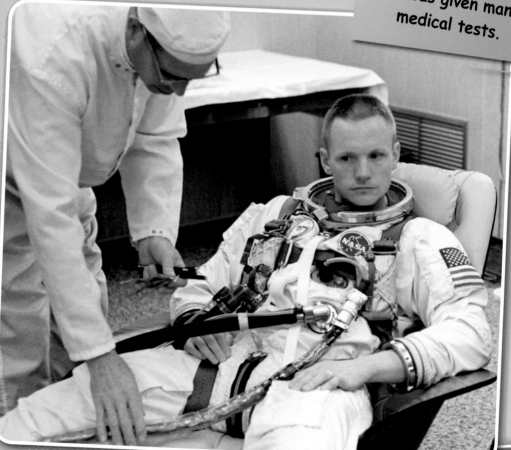

Armstrong was the **flight commander** on the *Gemini 8* flight. His aim was to link up with another spacecraft, but there were problems. *Gemini 8* had to return to Earth early.

In this photo, Armstrong is about to climb into *Gemini 8*. The other astronaut on the flight is behind him. Can you find out his name?

FACT CAT FACT

Altogether there were 10 Gemini flights. On the *Gemini 4* flight, an astronaut floated in space for the first time.

PROJECT APOLLO

In 1967, US scientists began making plans for a Moon landing. They designed a new spacecraft called Apollo. It had three parts: a **lunar module**, a **command module**, and a **service module**.

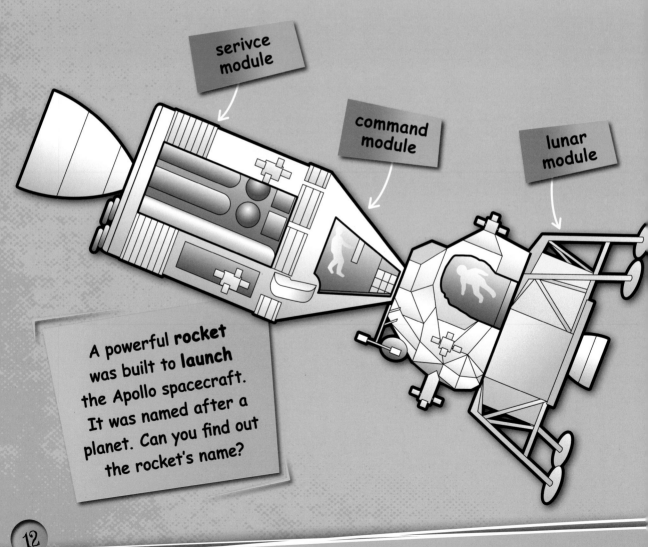

serivce module

command module

lunar module

A powerful **rocket** was built to **launch** the Apollo spacecraft. It was named after a planet. Can you find out the rocket's name?

There were many test flights before the Moon landing. *Apollo 8* carried astronauts around the Moon. *Apollo 9* tested the lunar module. *Apollo 10* flew to the Moon, but it did not land.

Apollo 11 was the first spacecraft to make a Moon landing. Neil Armstrong was the flight commander. Michael Collins was the command module pilot. Buzz Aldrin was the lunar module pilot.

Michael Collins

Neil Armstrong

Buzz Aldrin

FACT CAT FACT

The *Apollo 8* spacecraft reached a speed of 38,938 kilometres (24,200 miles) per hour. This was the fastest speed that humans had ever travelled.

APOLLO 11

On 16 July 1969, *Apollo 11* was launched. It took off from the Kennedy Space Center in Florida, USA.

Apollo 11 spacecraft

A gigantic rocket blasted *Apollo 11* into space. Then the rocket fell away and the spacecraft began to **orbit** the Earth.

FACT CAT FACT

Rocket launches can be very risky. In 1986, the spacecraft *Challenger* exploded soon after it was launched into space.

After one and a half orbits of the Earth, the **booster-rockets** on the service module were fired. *Apollo* travelled through space for three days. Then it began to orbit the Moon.

On July 20, the lunar module separated from the command module. It **descended** gently to the Moon. The lunar module was named after a bird. Can you find out its name?

WALKING ON THE MOON

Early in the morning of 21 July, Neil Armstrong stepped onto the Moon. Buzz Aldrin followed him 20 minutes later.

Armstrong took this photo of Aldrin on the Moon. The lunar module is behind him.

Instead of walking on the Moon, the astronauts bounced! This is because the pull of **gravity** is very weak on the Moon.

Sea of Tranquility

The lunar module landed in a part of the Moon called the Sea of Tranquility. What does the word 'tranquillity' mean?

FACT CAT FACT

The pull of gravity on the Moon is about one sixth as strong as it is on Earth. If you weigh 60 pounds (27 kg) on Earth, you will weigh 10 pounds (5 kg) on the Moon.

RETURN TO EARTH

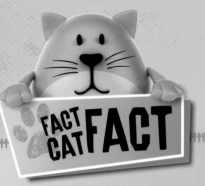

After two and a half hours on the Moon, the astronauts returned to the lunar module. Then it took off and connected with the command module. Booster-rockets sent the command module back to Earth.

command module

The command module splashed down in the Pacific Ocean. It floated on a rubber raft. Divers arrived in a boat to help the astronauts.

raft

The astronauts were taken to a large ship. They were kept in an **airtight cabin** for 18 days. They stayed there in case they had picked up any harmful **germs**.

The US President visited the astronauts in their cabin. Can you find out the President's name?

HORNET + 3

AFTER APOLLO 11

Apollo 11 was Armstrong's last space flight. But the Apollo Project ran for three more years. There were five more landings on the Moon.

lunar roving vehicle

Astronauts on *Apollo 17* were the last humans to visit the Moon. How long did they stay there?

After Armstrong left the Space Program, he became a teacher in a university. He also worked for many American companies. He died in 2012, at the age of 82.

Today, there are stations in space where astronauts can live for months. Modern astronauts are still **inspired** by Neil Armstrong, the first man on the Moon.

space station

FACT CAT FACT

Scientists have made some robot astronauts. In the future, these robots might even visit the Moon!

QUIZ

Try to answer the questions below. Look back through the book to help you. Check your answers on page 24.

1 There is no oxygen on the Moon. True or not true?

a) true

b) not true

2 How old was Armstrong when he started learning to fly a plane?

a) 25

b) 18

c) 15

3 Who was the first woman to travel in space?

a) Sally Ride

b) Valentina Tereshkova

c) Amelia Earhart

4 What was the name of the space project that sent Armstrong to the Moon?

a) Project Venus

b) Project Jupiter

c) Project Apollo

5 The command module of *Apollo 11* landed on the Moon. True or not true?

a) true

b) not true

GLOSSARY

airtight cabin a very small room that is sealed tightly so no germs can get in or out

astronaut someone who travels in space

award a badge, a medal or a prize given as a reward for achieving something good

booster-rocket a rocket that launches an object into space

command module the part of a spacecraft that carries the astronauts through space

compete to try to do better than somebody else

descend to move downwards

flight commander the person in charge of a flight

germs very small living things that cause diseases

gravity the force that pulls things down towards the surface of the Earth

inspire to encourage someone to do something

launch to send a spacecraft up into space

licence a document giving permission to do something

lunar module the part of a spacecraft that can land on the Moon

mankind all the people on Earth

navy ships and sailors that defend a country at sea. In modern times, a navy includes planes that take off from ships.

orbit to travel around the Earth, the Moon, or a planet

oxygen a colourless gas found in the air, that humans and animals need in order to breathe

pilot someone who flies an aircraft or a spacecraft

rocket a vehicle shaped like a tube with a pointed end that can travel very fast through the air

service module the part of a spacecraft that contains booster-rockets and other important equipment used in the flight. It burns up before the spacecraft returns to Earth.

Space Program a set of journeys and experiments that aim to explore space

Space Race the competition between the USA and Russia in the 1950s and 1960s, in which they both tried to be the first to achieve important goals in space travel

university a place where people go to study

INDEX

ANSWERS

Pages 4–20

page 4: Armstrong's Moon walk lasted for two hours and 36 minutes.

page 7: Orville Wright made the first successful aeroplane flight in 1903.

page 9: Yuri Gagarin's spacecraft was called *Vostok 1.*

page 11: David Scott was the other astronaut on *Gemini 8.*

page 12: The Apollo launch rocket was called *Saturn.*

page 15: The lunar module of *Apollo 11* was called *Eagle.*

page 17: The word 'tranquility' means calmness or peacefulness. The Sea of Tranquility was given its name in 1651.

page 19: President Richard Nixon visited the astronauts of *Apollo 11.*

page 20: Astronauts from *Apollo 17* stayed on the Moon for three days.

Quiz answers

1   a) true
2   c) Armstrong was 15 when he had his first flying lessons.
3   b) Valentina Tereshkova
4   c) Project Apollo
5   b) not true. It was the lunar module of *Apollo 11* that landed on the Moon.